8/17

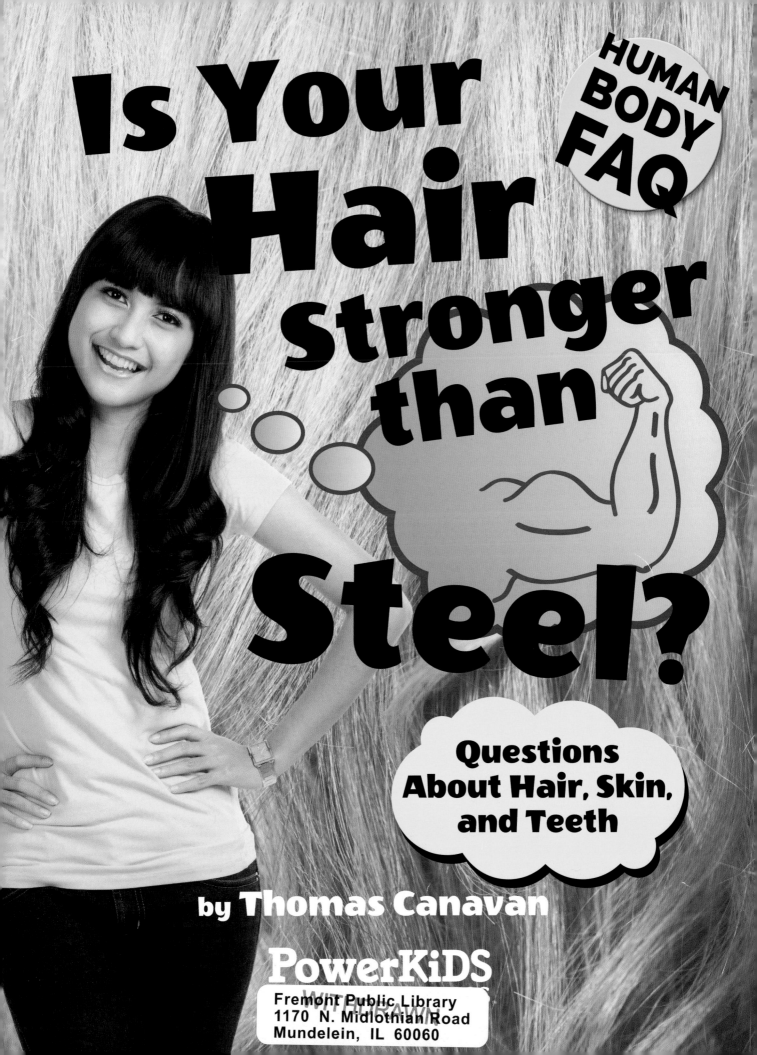

Is Your Hair Stronger than Steel?

HUMAN BODY FAQ

Questions About Hair, Skin, and Teeth

by **Thomas Canavan**

PowerKiDS

Published in 2017 by **The Rosen Publishing Group, Inc.**
29 East 21st Street, New York, NY 10010

Cataloging-in-Publication Data

Names: Canavan, Thomas.
Title: Is your hair stronger than steel? / Thomas Canavan.
Description: New York : PowerKids Press, 2017. | Series: Human body FAQ | Includes index.
Identifiers: ISBN 9781499431681 (pbk.) | ISBN 9781499432244 (library bound) |
  ISBN 9781499431698 (6 pack)
Subjects: LCSH: Hair--Juvenile literature. | Skin--Juvenile literature. | Teeth--Juvenile literature.
Classification: LCC QP88.3 C317 2017 | DDC 612.7'99--dc23

Author: Thomas Canavan
Designers: Supriya Sahai and Emma Randall
Editors: Joe Harris and Anna Brett

Picture credits: Cover illustration: Shutterstock. Interior illustrations: Shutterstock

Manufactured in the United States of America
CPSIA Compliance Information: Batch #BW17PK: For Further Information contact Rosen Publishing, New York, New York at 1-800-237-9932.

Contents

Why do we need skin and hair?

Your "outer wrapping" of skin, hair, teeth, and nails does a lot more than keep up appearances. Between them, they protect you from damage or infection and keep you at the right temperature. You can become seriously ill if you get too hot or too cold. Your skin acts as a blanket against the cold and allows heat to escape when you're hot.

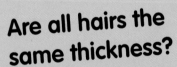

Are all hairs the same thickness?

Generally speaking, East Asian people have thicker individual hairs than people from other parts of the world.

Is your hair stronger than steel?

An object of around 3 ounces (100 g) could dangle on a single strand of human hair. That's nearly two regular-sized bars of soap! It's not quite as strong as steel, but it's up there with other strong substances like Kevlar, used to make bulletproof vests.

Bacteria, yuck!

Why do hairs really stand on end?
Your body hairs lie flat when you're hot and rise when you're cold to trap a warming "blanket" of air.

How does skin protect you from germs?

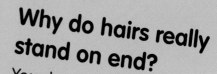

Think about all the germs in the air, and on the things you touch. Your skin shields your organs and major systems from the illnesses that those germs can cause. Just a small break in your skin can provide an opening for infection. That's why your body works quickly to form a scab over a cut. It plugs the hole so that new skin can grow.

How thick is your skin?

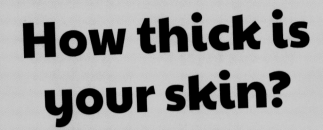

I t differs in thickness around your body. The thickest skin is on the soles of your feet, and is around 0.16 inch (4 mm) thick. Your eyelids are made of some of your thinnest skin, only 0.02 inch (0.5 mm) thick. Your skin does lots of different jobs, from protecting and insulating your body to giving you the sense of touch.

Thinnest skin!

Is skin really an organ?

Yes—the largest of the body's organs. Laid flat, a 13-year-old's skin would cover around 18 square feet (1.7 sq m)—about the size of a twin bed.

Thickest skin!

How does skin work?

It is divided into layers. The part that you can see, called the epidermis, is the outside layer. It forms the protective barrier for your body. The layer beneath is the dermis, which contains blood vessels, sweat glands, and hair follicles. The bottom layer, called the hypodermis, connects your skin with your muscles.

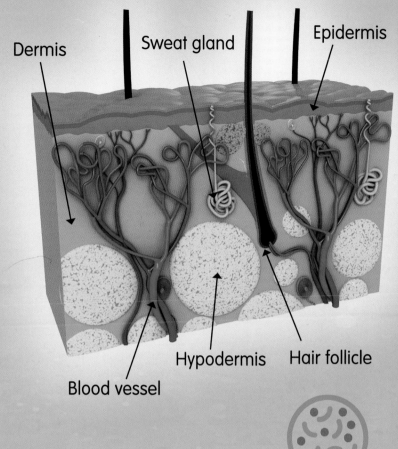

Dermis

Sweat gland

Epidermis

Hypodermis

Hair follicle

Blood vessel

How much dead skin comes off?

Every minute you lose 30,000 to 40,000 dead cells from the surface of your skin.

Yikes!

Are we really covered by dead skin?

The skin that you see is made up of dead skin cells. New cells are constantly forming at the base of the epidermis. They then begin the journey upward. Older cells, nearer the surface, die, and rise to the surface as these new cells replace them.

Epidermis

Why do we get scabs on our skin?

When the skin is cut or grazed, your body works fast to repair it. Special cells in your blood called platelets work with a protein called fibrin to form a scab. The scab keeps germs out of your body while new skin is growing underneath. Once the new skin has grown, the scab falls off. If the cut was large, you may get a scar. Scars are generally a lighter color than the rest of the skin, and don't have hair.

Can you have too much skin?

Skin is like an elastic band. If you stretch it out for a long time you'll create more of it that won't just disappear again. People who lose weight quickly sometimes have too much skin for their smaller bodies.

8

Why does skin change color in the sun?

Cells in the outer layer of your skin make a pigment called melanin that gives your skin its natural tone. The darker your skin, the more melanin it contains. The sun makes your body produce more melanin to protect it from harmful rays, which in turn makes your skin darker and gives you a temporary "tan."

Why does skin sweat?

Your skin keeps you cool by bringing water to the surface. As the water evaporates, it takes away heat.

Can your skin really turn red and green?

When blood rushes to your face you might look redder than normal—this is called blushing. When you feel sick all the blood is directed to your stomach, so your blue veins show through your yellow skin to make it look green!

Why do people have different color hair?

Hair color is controlled by your genes, meaning it is decided before you are born. Two different types of melanin combine to produce the particular shade of blonde, brown, red or black hair that you have.

What happens when you dye your hair?
The outer layer of your hair is protected by scale-like cuticles, which can open or close. A chemical in permanent hair dye called ammonia opens the cuticles, so that the dye can stain your hair.

Why does hair turn gray?

As you get older, the cells that produce the color in your hair follicle begin to die. This means that the hair follicle becomes a more transparent color like gray, silver or white. People generally start getting gray hairs in their mid-30s.

How quickly does hair grow?

Don't worry if you don't like your new haircut—hair grows around 0.5 inch (1.2 cm) each month so you'll soon have new hair to play with.

Why is my hair curly?

The shape of your hair is determined by the shape of your follicle. If you have curly hair your follicle will be flat. If you have straight hair your follicle is circular. All hair twists as it grows, but the more twists, the more curl your hair will have!

Why don't women have beards?

Facial hair was common in our ancestors, but now it's absent in most women. The difference seems to be because of evolution. Humans have become less hairy over millions of years. Over time, men came to prefer women with little or no facial hair. Those women would pass on this "hairless" gene to their daughters. Then those women would have the head start in the ancient dating game.

How fast do beards grow?

Most body hair grows at the same rate: about 0.5 inch (1.2 cm) a month. The average man spends 60 hours shaving each year.

Why don't boys shave?

Boys' bodies begin to change as they become adults. Many of those changes are caused by hormones (chemicals produced by the body). One of those hormones, called testosterone, builds up muscles, makes boys' voices get deeper, and causes hair to begin growing on the face and on other parts of the body.

How long can a beard grow?

The longest beard ever measured stretched 17.5 feet (5.33 m).

Why aren't the palms of our hands hairy?

Even the furriest, hairiest mammals have no hair follicles on the palms of their hands or soles of their feet. Hairs would be worn away by the constant contact with the ground, and would make it more difficult to grip onto things.

Why don't women go bald?

Women may not have beards, but they normally keep the hair on the top of their head all their life. For the same reason that men have beards, it's because of hormones. The male hormone testosterone can make hair follicles shrivel up until no more hair grows. Although women produce some testosterone, their female hormones protect their hair.

Keratin!

What is hair made of?

Hair is mostly made up of a protein called keratin. It is the same substance that makes your fingernails and toenails. It is also what animals' hooves, claws, horns, and even feathers and beaks are made of.

14

What is a follicle?
Each of your 100,000 hairs grows from its own follicle, a tiny organ in the dermis layer of your skin.

Can women ever lose their hair?

As girls mature, their bodies start to produce hormones that will help them have babies. These are the female hormones that protect their hair. Women stop producing these hormones when they're too old to have babies. Their hair can become thinner, and even disappear. Some women may lose their hair completely if their hormones are affected by something out of the ordinary. That could be an illness, a shock, or even having a baby.

How long do hairs last?
The average life-span of a human hair is 2–7 years. Then it is replaced.

Why do we have eyebrows?

Eyebrows might seem like an afterthought, added once human faces were designed. But they serve some practical purposes in protecting you. Their location just above your eyes makes them ideal guards for two of your most delicate organs. Plus—as you probably know--they are an excellent way of communicating emotions.

What if you had no eyebrows?

You can simply look at a mannequin in a store window to see how odd you'd look. But eyebrows have an important job to do—diverting sweat, rain, and other liquids from flowing into your eyes. Together with your eyelashes, which catch dust and other objects, they protect your sense of sight.

Can eyebrows speak?

Eyebrows are an important part of nonverbal communication—the type that doesn't involve words or even sounds. Most of us can judge another person's mood by first looking at their facial expression. Eyebrows are especially good at revealing your emotions—whether you're sad, angry, happy, or surprised.

How do eyebrows move?

There are over 30 muscles in the head and face, which help you frown, smile, and raise your eyebrows in surprise.

What if you pluck your eyebrows?

Your eyebrows can grow back, but they're the slowest-growing hairs on your body.

Why do we get chapped lips?

Your lips lack sweat glands, so they don't produce natural oils to stop them from drying out. Lips are also covered with a much thinner layer of skin than the rest of your body. This makes them more sensitive (and explains the fact that lips are usually a different shade from the rest of your face, as the blood vessels are nearer the surface).

Why do lips tingle?

There are lots of nerve endings near the surface of the skin. Lips react to some spices just as they would if they were being tickled!

How many muscles do lips use?

A simple action like blowing a trumpet uses a set of four muscles around the mouth.

Do we really need our lips to live?

One of the very first things you did—apart from crying—was to suckle, or pucker your lips to take in milk. This basic action, or instinct, allows you to get essential nourishment. Your lips continue to help you eat, sealing your mouth as you chew and swallow. They are also very sensitive to touch, which helps warn your body about danger.

My lips are sealed!

Why do lips make different shapes?

Lip muscles help you move food into your mouth and make sounds that others can hear. Your lips help you produce about half of the sounds that you need to speak. Try saying "My big mouth" without closing your lips! They also seal your mouth closed to keep out water or dirt.

Why do we grow two sets of teeth?

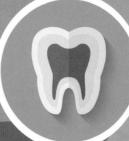

It might seem odd replacing a full set of teeth, but your first set of baby (or milk) teeth has done its job by the time you're five or six years old. They've helped you chew and get important nourishment while your body prepares to house a larger—and stronger—set as an adult.

CHOMP! CHOMP!

Are adult teeth tougher than baby teeth?

No, they're just bigger! Your 20 baby teeth do their job very well, allowing you to slice, cut, and grind food. But you need more teeth to fill your larger, adult jaw. The first set helps your jaw grow in a way that will let your second set replace that first set—and still have room for the 12 extra teeth that adults have.

What are wisdom teeth?

Most people also have a third set of teeth—four molars called "wisdom teeth" that arrive when you're about 20.

Tough AND wise, huh?!

How does your first set know when to fall out?

That second set of teeth starts to develop while your first set is in place. When they're ready, they push through the jaw. Along the way, they dissolve the roots of the first set. Without those roots to anchor them, the baby teeth become loose.

What makes teeth so strong?

The outer layer of your teeth is covered in enamel, the hardest tissue in your body.

What causes a toothache?

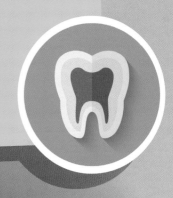

A toothache is a sign that something is wrong inside or near one of your teeth. It's mainly the result of dental decay—bits of a tooth being eaten away to allow germs to get inside. Luckily you can reduce the chance of developing a toothache with good habits like regular daily brushing.

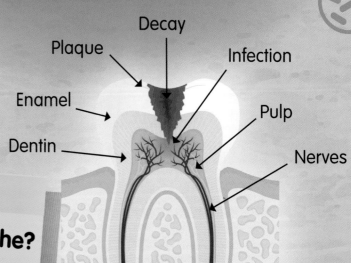

Plaque

Decay

Infection

Enamel

Pulp

Dentin

Nerves

How serious is a toothache?
Severe tooth decay can kill you! Historians believe that ancient Egypt's pharaoh, Ramses II, died of a toothache.

Why is a toothache so painful?

Plaque, a sticky substance containing lots of bacteria, constantly forms around your teeth. Sugars from food mix with the bacteria, releasing acid. It can eat through the outer layer of your teeth and cause cavities, or holes. Germs enter through these cavities, eating away at the inside of your teeth. The pain is a signal from the nerves in the affected area.

What if an adult tooth falls out?

If it gets knocked out whole, a dentist may be able to set it back in place. Keep it in milk and get it looked at immediately.

How can we prevent a toothache?

Regular brushing helps prevent germs from collecting and attacking your teeth. And you should try not to have too many sugary foods or drinks because they can eat away at the enamel covering of your teeth, opening the way for painful infection.

Why don't humans have claws?

What are the white spots on nails?

Small white marks are no big deal—you may have knocked or bent the nail. But nails can show how healthy you are—if they're darker or have patches on them, you might be unwell.

Most mammals have sharp claws to help them dig or to attack other animals. Primates, the group of mammals that includes monkeys, apes, and humans, have nails instead. As primates developed, claws became smaller and flatter. These smaller versions, nails, are better for handling small objects, such as nuts and fruit, and working with tools—something that other mammals rarely do.

Why don't fingernails sweat?

Nails are made of keratin (like hair). This protein is strong and can either be flexible (like hair) or solid (like nails or animal claws and horns). The bits you can see are no longer growing—they are made of dead cells—and so they don't sweat. The growing takes place on the skin underneath the hard nail.

Why do nails grow so fast?

Fingernails protect the sensitive nerve endings of your fingertips. They may be strong, but they are easily chipped, broken, or worn away. They need to grow constantly to perform their task in life. On average, they grow about 0.14 inch (3.5 mm) per month. Toenails do the same job, but are subject to less wear and tear, so they grow at a slower rate—around 0.06 inch (1.6 mm) per month.

Is it bad to bite your nails?

Chewing on dirty nails can introduce germs into your body, and lead to infections if you damage the skin.

Crunchy!

Why do I have to shower?

Have people always washed?

Yes, even in ancient history. So you have no excuse for soap dodging! Ancient Rome's Baths of Caracalla could hold 1,600 bathers at the same time.

Your body has many ways of fighting back against illness and infection. But we can do a lot to help it fight off bacteria and viruses. Sensible cleaning habits, known as hygiene, helps remove those harmful germs—which are too small for us to see.

What is an infection?

"Microorganism" is the scientific name for the tiny, invisible germs all around us. Some of these bacteria and viruses are safe or even helpful. But harmful microorganisms can enter the body, where they multiply quickly and cause illnesses. Such an invasion is called an infection.

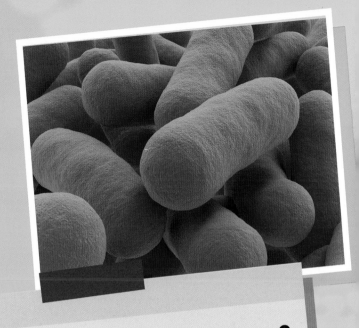

Can doing the laundry fight disease?

Washing can kill disease-carrying fleas and bedbugs living in dirty carpets and blankets.

What if your hands look clean?

It's important to wash your hands regularly, and especially before you eat. Because germs are small enough to be invisible, you might think that your hands are completely clean. But your hands are constantly touching other things—doorknobs, books, or other people's hands—and that contact transmits germs.

How does everything work together?

Our bodies are made up of different systems. Each system has its own function, such as converting food into energy, or removing waste. The systems all work together to bring the human body to life.

Circulatory system
Your heart is at the center of this system, which pumps blood around your body via veins and arteries.

Skeletal system
All 206 bones make up the skeletal system, which supports and protects your body.

Muscular system
Around 640 muscles in your body help you move. Your muscles are attached to your bones by tendons.

Respiratory system
Your lungs draw in air to bring oxygen into the body and push air out to move carbon dioxide out.

Nervous system
The brain passes messages around the body via a system of nerves. Nerves also pass messages received by your senses back to the brain.

Excretory system
Toxins and waste materials are removed from your body by this system, which includes your kidneys and bladder.

Testes (male)

Digestive system
This system takes in food, and breaks it down into energy and basic nutrients the body can use.

Endocrine system
Glands in this system produce chemicals called hormones that help you grow and change your mood.

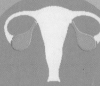

Ovaries (female)

29

Glossary

artery A tube in the circulatory system that transports oxygenated blood from the heart around the body.

bacteria Microscopic organisms made of one cell that can often survive in extreme conditions.

carbon dioxide A colorless, odorless gas produced when the human body respires and breathes out.

cell The smallest functioning unit in an organism. Cells join together to make tissue.

dermis The inner layer of your skin containing blood vessels, sweat glands, and hair follicles.

emotions Feelings such as happiness or anger that are affected by circumstance or mood.

enamel The hard outer layer that protects your teeth.

epidermis The thin outer layer of your skin.

evaporate To turn from a liquid into a vapor.

evolution The process by which living organisms change over many generations to become better adapted to their environment.

follicle A tube-shaped cavity that contains the root of a hair.

genes A sequence of molecules (in the form of DNA) that carries information about how an organism will appear and behave.

germ A microorganism that can produce disease in the body.

gland An organ in the body that releases chemicals for use in the body.

hormones Chemicals produced by the body that act like messengers.

hypodermis The bottom layer of the skin that connects it to your muscles.

infection When harmful microorganisms enter the body and multiply quickly, causing an illness.

mammals Warm-blooded vertebrate animals with hair or fur. They give birth to live young and produce milk to nourish them.

melanin The pigment that gives human skin, hair, and eyes their color.

molars The broad teeth at the back of the mouth that grind food.

nerves Fibers in the body that transmit messages around the body.

nourishment Food that enters the body and enables growth, health and sustenance.

organ A collection of cells that work together to perform a specific function.

oxygen A colorless, odorless gas found in the air that the body breathes in.

primates The group of mammals that includes monkeys, apes, and humans.

scab A crust that forms over an opening in your skin to protect new skin growing underneath.

temperature A degree of heat measured on a scale.

tendon The tissue that attaches muscle to a bone.

veins Tubes in the circulatory system that transport deoxygenated blood from the body back to the heart.

virus An organism smaller than bacteria that invades living cells and uses them to multiply and spread, causing illness.

Further Information

Further reading

Big Book of the Body *by Minna Lacey* (Usborne, 2016)

Body Works *by Anna Claybourne* (QED Publishing, 2014)

Everything You Need to Know about the Human Body *by Patricia MacNair* (Kingfisher, 2011)

Guinness World Records: Amazing Body Records *by Christa Roberts* (HarperCollins, 2016)

How the Body Works *by editors of DK* (Dorling Kindersley, 2016)

Project Science: Human Body *by Sally Hewitt* (Franklin Watts, 2012)

Websites

PowerKids Press has developed an online list of websites related to the subject of this book. This site is updated regularly. Please use this link to access the list: **www.powerkidslinks.com/hbfaq/hair**

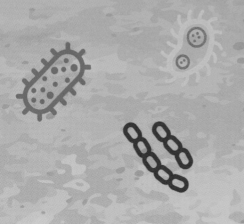

Index